Fearless

A 6-SESSION BIBLE STUDY

Angela Donadio

BRIDGE
LOGOS

Newberry, FL 32669

Bridge-Logos
Newberry, FL 32669

Fearless:
Ordinary Women of the Bible Who Dared to do Extraordinary Things
by Angela Donadio

Printed in the United States of America

Library of Congress Catalog Card Number: 2019932107

International Standard Book Number: 978-1-61036-401-0

Cover photo: Andrew Rich, istockphoto.com

Cover/Interior design: Kent Jensen, knail.com

VP 01 06/2019